Knock Knock Jokes

The big book of funny knock knock jokes

Table of Contents

Introduction 1

Knock Knock Jokes 2

Conclusion 39

Introduction

Thank you for choosing this book, full of the best knock knock jokes!

 The jokes within the following pages are suitable for all ages and will keep the whole family entertained for hours.

I hope you have fun trying to make your friends and family laugh with these funny knock knock jokes.

Once again, thanks for choosing this book, I hope you enjoy it!

Knock Knock Jokes

Knock knock.

Who's there?

Ach.

Ach who?

Bless you!

Knock knock.

Who's there?

Leaf.

Leaf who?

Leaf me alone!

Knock knock.

Who's there?

Nobel.

Nobel who?

No bell. That's why I knocked!

Knock knock.

Who's there?

Lettuce.

Lettuce who?

Lettuce in!

Knock knock.

Who's there?

Hawaii.

Hawaii who?

I'm good thanks, how are you?

Knock knock.

Who's there?

Who.

Who who?

What are you, an owl?!

Knock knock.

Who's there?

Anita.

Anita who?

Anita borrow some sugar.

Knock knock.

Who's there?

Orange.

Orange who?

Orange you going to open the door?

Knock knock.

Who's there?

Woo.

Woo who?

Don't get too excited, it's just a joke!

Knock knock.

Who's there?

Figs.

Figs who?

Figs the doorbell, it's broken!

Knock knock.

Who's there?

Annie.

Annie who?

Annie thing you can do I can do better!

Knock knock.

Who's there?

Boo.

Boo who?

Don't cry, it's just a joke!

Knock knock.

Who's there?

Theodore.

Theodore who?

Theodore is locked, please let me in!

Knock knock.

Who's there?

Amos.

Amos who?

A mosquito bit me!

Knock knock.

Who's there?

Police.

Police who?

Police let us in, it's cold out here!

Knock knock.

Who's there?

Beats.

Beats who?

Beats me!

Knock knock.

Who's there?

The interrupting cow.

The interrupting co-

Moooooooo!

Knock knock.

Who's there?

Yoda lady.

Yoda lady who?

Wow, I didn't know you could yodel!

Knock knock.

Who's there?

Deja.

Deja who?

Knock knock.

Knock knock.

Who's there?

Urine.

Urine who?

Urine trouble if you don't open the door!

Knock knock.

Who's there?

Kenya.

Kenya who?

Kenya open the door?

Knock knock.

Who's there?

Kanga.

Kanga who?

No, it's kangaroo!

Knock knock.

Who's there?

Spell.

Spell who?

W-H-O

Knock knock.

Who's there?

Owls say.

Owls say who?

Yep, they sure do!

Knock knock.

Who's there?

Cash.

Cash who?

No thanks, I prefer peanuts.

Knock knock.

Who's there?

Ida.

Ida who?

It's pronounced "Idaho", actually.

Knock knock.

Who's there?

Cook.

Cook who?

Yes, you are a little crazy!

Knock knock.

Who's there?

Cereal.

Cereal who?

Cereal pleasure to meet you.

Knock knock.

Who's there?

Harry.

Harry who?

Harry up and open the door!

Knock knock.

Who's there?

I scream.

I scream who?

I scream is my favorite food!

Knock knock.

Who's there?

Doris.

Doris who?

Doris locked, that's why I knocked.

Knock knock.

Who's there?

Tank.

Tank who?

You're welcome!

Knock knock.

Who's there?

Opportunity.

That's not possible! Opportunity doesn't knock twice!

Knock knock.

Who's there?

Iran.

Iran who?

Iran over here to see you.

Knock knock.

Who's there?

Amish.

Amish who?

Awh, I miss you too!

Knock knock.

Who's there?

A little girl.

A little girl who?

A little girl who can't reach the doorbell!

Knock knock.

Who's there?

Doctor.

Doctor who?

That's a great TV show, isn't it!

Knock knock.

Who's there?

Gorilla.

Gorilla who?

Gorilla me a hamburger, please!

Knock knock.

Who's there?

Dumbbell.

Dumbbell who?

Dumbbell doesn't work so I had to knock!

Knock knock.

Who's there?

A pile up.

A pile up who?

Ewww, that's gross!

Knock knock.

Who's there?

Pencil.

Pencil who?

Pencil fall down if you don't wear a belt!

Knock knock.

Who's there?

Alex.

Alex who?

Alex the questions around here!

Knock knock.

Who's there?

Daisy.

Daisy who?

Daisy me rollin', they hatin'!

Knock knock.

Who's there?

Frank.

Frank who?

Frank you for being my friend!

Knock knock.

Who's there?

Wooden shoe.

Wooden shoe who?

Wooden shoe like to know!

Knock knock.

Who's there?

Cows go.

Cows go who?

No silly, cows go moo!

Knock knock.

Who's there?

Justin.

Justin who?

Justin time for lunch!

Knock knock.

Who's there?

Mikey.

Mikey who?

Mikey doesn't work, could you let me in?

Knock knock.

Who's there?

Olive.

Olive who?

Olive right next to you.

Knock knock.

Who's there?

Dishes.

Dishes who?

Dishes me, who are you?

Knock knock.

Who's there?

Luke.

Luke who?

Luke through the keyhole and see for yourself!

Knock knock.

Who's there?

Broccoli.

Broccoli who?

Broccoli doesn't have a last name!

Knock knock.

Who's there?

Olive.

Olive who.

Olive you!

Knock knock.

Who's there?

Leena.

Leena who?

Leena little closer and I'll tell you.

Knock knock.

Who's there?

Keith.

Keith who?

Keith your hands off of me!

Knock knock.

Who's there?

Some.

Some who?

Someone trying to tell a knock knock joke.

Knock knock.

Who's there?

Canoe.

Canoe who?

Canoe come outside?

Knock knock.

Who's there?

Honeybee.

Honeybee who?

Honeybee a dear and open the door.

Knock knock.

Who's there?

A broken pencil.

A broken pencil who?

Never mind, it's pointless.

Knock knock.

Who's there?

Double.

Double who?

W!

Knock knock.

Who's there?

I am.

I am who?

You don't know who you are?

Knock knock.

Who's there?

Iva.

Iva who?

Iva sore hand from knocking!

Knock knock.

Who's there?

Merry.

Merry who?

Merry Christmas!

Knock knock.

Who's there?

Orange.

Orange who?

Orange you going to let me in?

Knock knock.

Who's there?

Dozen.

Dozen who?

Dozen anyone want to open the door?

Knock knock.

Who's there?

Henrietta.

Henrietta who?

Henrietta ate a worm that was in his apple.

Knock knock.

Who's there?

Harry.

Harry who?

Harry up, it's cold out here!

Knock knock.

Who's there?

A herd.

A herd who?

A herd you were home so I came over!

Knock knock.

Who's there?

Adore.

Adore who?

Adore is between us, so open up!

Knock knock.

Who's there?

Noah.

Noah who?

Noah good place we can go for lunch?

Knock knock.

Who's there?

Dwayne.

Dwayne who?

Dwayne the bathtub, it's overflowing!

Knock knock.

Who's there?

Robin.

Robin who?

Robin you! Give me your money!

Knock knock.

Who's there?

Howard.

Howard who?

Howard I know?!

Knock knock.

Who's there?

I eat mop.

I eat mop who?

That's disgusting!

Knock knock.

Who's there?

Sadie.

Sadie who?

Sadie magic word and I'll leave.

Knock knock.

Who's there?

Hike.

Hike who?

I didn't know you liked Japanese poetry!

Knock knock.

Who's there?

Cargo.

Cargo who?

Cargo beep beep.

Knock knock.

Who's there?

Ice cream soda.

Ice cream soda who?

Ice cream soda people can hear me!

Knock knock.

Who's there?

To.

To who?

Actually, it's "to whom."

Knock knock.

Who's there?

Candice.

Candice who?

Candice joke get any worse?

Knock knock.

Who's there?

Haven.

Haven who?

Haven you heard enough of these knock knock jokes?

Knock knock.

Who's there?

Nun.

Nun who?

Nun of your business!

Knock knock.

Who's there?

Oscar.

Oscar who?

Oscar silly question, get a silly answer!

Knock knock.

Who's there?

Conrad.

Conrad who?

Conrad-ulations!

Knock knock.

Who's there?

Mustache.

Mustache who?

Mustache you a question, but I'm shaving it for later!

Knock knock.

Who's there?

Ya.

Ya who?

No, Google is better!

Knock knock.

Who's there?

Control freak.

Control fre-

Okay now you say "control freak who".

Knock knock.

Who's there?

Billy Joe Jenkins.

Billy Joe Jenkins who?

Jeez, how many people named Billy Joe Jenkins do you know?!

Knock knock.

Who's there?

Europe.

Europe who?

No, you're a poo!

Knock knock.

Who's there?

Cabbage.

Cabbage who?

You really expect cabbage to have a last name?

Knock knock.

Who's there?

Razor.

Razor who?

Razor hands, this is a stick up!

Knock knock.

Who's there?

Sweden.

Sweden who?

Sweden sour chicken.

Knock knock.

Who's there?

Art.

Art who?

R2-D2.

Knock knock.

Who's there?

Voodoo.

Voodoo who?

Voodoo you think you are asking all these questions!

Knock knock.

Who's there?

Says.

Says who?

Says me, that's who!

Knock knock.

Who's there?

Amish.

Amish who?

Really, you're a shoe? Okay then...

Knock knock.

Who's there?

A Mayan.

A Mayan who?

A Mayan the way?

Knock knock.

Who's there?

Tennis.

Tennis who?

Tennis five plus five.

Knock knock.

Who's there?

Snow.

Snow who?

Snow use, I forgot my name again.

Knock knock.

Who's there?

Nicholas.

Nicholas who?

Nicholas not that much these days.

Knock knock.

Who's there?

Abby.

Abby who?

Abby birthday to you!

Knock knock.

Who's there?

Alfie.

Alfie who?

Alfie terrible if you don't let me in.

Knock knock.

Who's there?

Armageddon.

Armageddon who?

Armageddon a little bored, let's go out!

Knock knock.

Who's there?

Barbara.

Barbara who?

Barbara black sheep have you any wool…

Knock knock.

Who's there?

Burglar.

Burglar who?

Burglars don't knock!

Knock knock.

Who's there?

CD.

CD who?

CD guy on your doorstep?

Knock knock.

Who's there?

Claire.

Claire who?

Claire the way, I'm coming through!

Knock knock.

Who's there?

Egg.

Egg who?

Eggcited to see me?

Knock knock.

Who's there?

Europe.

Europe who?

Europe early this morning!

Knock knock.

Who's there?

Fangs.

Fangs who?

Fangs for letting me in!

Conclusion

Thanks again for choosing this book!

I hope you had fun sharing these jokes with your friends and family.

If you enjoyed this book, please keep an eye out for my other titles available on Amazon as well as other book retailers around the world!

www.ingramcontent.com/pod-product-compliance
Lightning Source LLC
LaVergne TN
LVHW021743060526
838200LV00052B/3436